# HOW CURIOUS?

With millions of animal species on Earth, how do you choose which ones qualify as *Curious Critters*? For me, the decision is easy: *they all do*. Animals always intrigue me. In this book, the first of a series, I have collected portraits of a range of remarkable, bizarre, and often amusing creatures commonly found throughout North America—some in nearby woodlands, some in local lakes, some in your own back yard, and, yes, some inside your house, invited or *not*.

I am grateful that these animals posed for portraits, allowing me to depict for you their unique colors, textures, shapes, and seeming *personalities*. I hope that white backgrounds, which eliminate distractions, help you notice clues about the animals' behaviors, diets, life cycles, and habitats. Learning about one animal can lead to learning about others. So, as you peruse these portraits of Curious Critters—and listen to their chatter—ask lots of questions. Then seek lots of answers. *The curious always learn*.

**For Sarah and Phoebe**

All animals portrayed in this book were handled carefully and not sedated. Some resided at centers dedicated to education, conservation, and rehabilitation. Wild animals were returned safely to their habitats.

Additional Curious Critters: cedar waxwing, front jacket flap; scorpion fly, page 1; Gila monster (Toledo Zoo), pages 2–3; firefly, page 32; question mark butterfly, back jacket flap; great spangled fritillary butterfly, spicebush swallowtail butterfly, and tiger swallowtail butterfly, spine (top to bottom).

FitzSimmons, David. Curious critters / text & photography by David FitzSimmons. p. cm. Includes index.

SUMMARY: A variety of animals common to North America pose for portraits against a white background while narrating distinctive aspects of their natural histories.

LCCN 2011925529    ISBN-13: 978-193660769-3    ISBN-10: 193660769-7
1. Animals—North America—Juvenile literature.    [1. Animals—North America.]
I. Title.    QL151.F58 2011    591.9'7    QBI11-600072

Printed by Reliance Printing (Shenzhen) Co. Ltd.
Shenzhen, China.
Job # HN 2011 - 0012

First Edition, September 2011
10 9 8 7 6 5 4 3 2 1
Printed in China

## SIGMA

**All photographs in this book were produced with SIGMA lenses.**
To learn more about the photographic techniques and equipment used in making this book, please visit *www.curious-critters.com*.

# CURIOUS CRITTERS™

Text and Photography by
## David FitzSimmons

WILD IRIS
PUBLISHING
BELLVILLE, OHIO

# AMERICAN BULLFROG

*R–r–r–u–m. R–r–r–u–m. R–r–r–u–m. R–r–r–u–m.*

I love sitting by the edge of the pond and singing all day long. I sing for the lady frogs.
Sometimes I climb onto land, but there's nothing like leaping . . . *splash!* . . . back into the water.

I love water. It keeps my skin looking good—wet and slimy!

# AMERICAN TOAD

It's just not true: I don't give people warts when they touch me.

And that fairy tale about a princess kissing a frog . . . *Bah!* It's rubbish!
Why wouldn't anyone want to kiss a toad?

Okay, so I might not be the most handsome critter, but I make a
beautiful trilling call. I quietly eat all kinds of annoying insects.
I stay out of the way, hiding in the leaves and dirt.
And I don't make a big show of leaping like those
frogs with their splashy dives. I humbly hop.

Hop.    Hop.    Hop.

# BLUE JAY

*Kee-eeeee-arr. Kee-eeeee-arr.*
*Ha!* I scared you with my hawk call, didn't I? You thought
I was coming to get you. Actually, I'm just a jabbering jay,
but I love to imitate hawks and other birds.

In the wild, I love to jabber.
*Jaay-jaay. Jaay-jaay.*
*Tool-ool. Tool-ool.*
*Wheed-le-ee. Wheed-le-ee.*
*Click, click, click.*

*Kee-eeeee-arr. Kee-eeeee-arr.*
*Ha!* Got you again. Not a hawk,
just me—a jabbering jay!

# OHIO CRAWFISH

Do you know why I'm waving my giant claws?
I'm warning you: Don't come any closer.

*Snap!    Snap!    Snap!*

I catch my food with these claws. I also attack and defend
myself with them.

*Snap!    Snap!    Snap!*

Do you want to know something
really cool?  If any of my legs get
hurt, including my giant claws, I
can grow new ones. Pretty neat, huh?
Now, enough chitchat. Back off!

*Snap!    Snap!    Snap!*

# GOLDFISH

*O-ooooh! Hello-ooooo!* It's good to see you! I do like visitors. Let's play a game: I'll flip my fins and swim around in this aquarium, and you throw in some food. Sound good? Great!

*O-ooooh* . . . well . . . those funny fish flakes are okay, but how about some veggies? A few green peas sound good. Or maybe you could find a few insects or worms or—*the guy on the previous page is not going to like this*—how about some baby crayfish?

Uh-oh. Here he comes. Sorry, crabby crayfish! Put those giant claws away!

Fish flakes are fine for me.

# SOUTHERN FLYING SQUIRREL

Yes. I can fly. Just a second. Okay. I spread my legs. *Wait!* Yes. I'm a bit jumpy.
Jittery. *Owls hunt me!* You see?

So. I climb a tree, go out on a limb, and jump.
Flaps of skin. Between my legs.
I spread them.
Then I gracefully

       G
           L
               I
                   D
                      E  .   .   .

Sleep? Me? No, *never!* Well, okay.
During the day. Inside a hollow tree.

Gotta fly. *Bye!*

# BIG BROWN BAT

*Gliding?* The little squirrel calls that flying? It's more like a long leap.

I can *really* fly. I have skin stretched across my fingers forming wings like a bird's. My wings allow me to fly up and down, left and right, wherever I want.

Now, stop looking and turn off the lights. I fly in the dark. I squeak and listen, squeak and listen. As my sounds bounce off objects, I hear where things are. It's called *echolocation*. Do you know what shapes I love to hear? Tasty beetles, juicy moths, and stinky bugs. I eat 'em as I fly.

During the day, leave me alone. Upside down, wrapped in my wings, I need my sleep!

# FOX SNAKE

Silently, silently, I sneak up on animals.
I wiggle in wetlands, slip through grass,
and climb up trees. In marshes and fields,
I look for rodents. Among branches, I find
birds and their eggs. That makes me hungry.

I am a constrictor.

I slither.

I squeeze.

*Sssssssssssssssssssssssssssssssssssssssssssss!*

# EASTERN SCREECH-OWL

*Waaah!* What woke me up? Sorry, I was sound asleep. I was up hunting all night.

How do I find food in the dark? Well, my big eyes help me see at night, and my big ears pick up the slightest sounds.

Listen! Did you hear that?

What was I saying?
Oh, yes, (let's whisper)
I search for rodents, bats,
birds, fish, and reptiles.
Last night's hunt was
so successful: I caught
a mouse and a snake.

It was nice sitting with
you for a moment,
but please excuse me.
I must see about getting
more sleep. . . .

# GRAY TREEFROG

I know, you're thinking, *gray? You look green*. Actually,
I change colors. Sometimes I'm almost black, other times
bright green, and often somewhere in between.

Do you know why I change colors?

It's kind of like hide-and-seek. Animals try
to find me—but not for play. They want
to eat me. So, I change colors to match
my surroundings. I camouflage myself.
If I'm among leaves, I turn green.
If I'm on bark, I'm harder to see
when I'm gray.

Do you know how I climb straight up?
On my feet I have sticky disks that
help me crawl up nearly anything.
You might even find me on
one of your windows!

# BUSH KATYDID

Sometimes I wish I could change color. I mean, all the other katydids
are green, but I'm pink. Scientists say that pink katydids are special.
My mother thinks so, too. She says that her great-great-great grandmother
was pink. That's how I got my color. It was handed down to me from my
relatives. I guess each of us shares traits with our relatives . . . the color of
our eyes, the shape of our noses, even the size of our feet!

My bright color is often pretty cool.
I blend in with pink flowers, and,
when I can't hide, it seems that birds
and other animals decide not to eat me.
I guess you could look at it this way:
*Would you eat a blue hamburger?*

# VIRGINIA OPOSSUM

I wrote a little poem, but I'm afraid to read it to you. What if you don't like it?

You really want to hear it? All right, here goes . . .

*Ode to Opossum*
*by O. Possum*

*Opossum! Opossum! How I love you!*
*You carry your kids like marsupials do.*
*Whenever you're bothered, you run on ahead.*
*If further provoked, you pretend you are dead.*
*But what I was wondering in writing these lines*
*is why say "Opossum," Possum? No "O" is fine!*

# CHINESE PRAYING MANTIS

I wasn't doing anything. I was just, uh, getting ready to . . . pray. Yeah, that's it.
Pray. Just folding my pointy, sharp front legs to . . .

All right, you got me. I was not going to pray. I was going to *prey*, P-R-*E*-Y.
That's right, I was looking for animals to eat.

Here's how I do it. See my back? What do my wing covers look like?
Exactly: They look like leaves. I hide among plants and then jump out,
grabbing insects and occasionally small reptiles, amphibians, and birds.
The sharp spines on my front legs help me hold my prey.

And, yes, it's true, mantids eat other mantids.
What? You think that's in bad taste?

Well, if you'll excuse me, I have
to get back to my preying!

# JUMPING SPIDER

Hey, there! I saw you coming. Eight times. Yep! That's right. I have eight eyes,
some on the back of my head. I can see in eight different directions at the same time.

Watch this. *Thwip!* Quite a jump, huh? *Thwip!*

Do you know how I jump? I don't have muscles like you. I have liquid inside me. I change
the pressure of the fluid in each of my eight legs, and that makes me move. I can jump long distances.

$T-H-W-I-P!$

$T-H-W-I-P!$

$T-H-W-I-P!$

See ya!

# RED FLAT BARK BEETLE

Oh, am I glad to see you! My back is getting *mite*-y itchy. Even though I crawl back and forth under the bark of trees, annoying little arachnids keep hanging onto me. You do see them, don't you?

Mites. That's what they are, with eight legs . . . which they don't seem to use much. They just hang onto me and ride. They might as well be shouting all along the tree, "Here comes the *big red bus!*"

To be truthful, they don't really hurt me, but—*oooooh!*—they are *mite*-y annoying!

# BLACK SWALLOWTAIL

I am beautiful, and I want to be seen. I take flight, showing off my beautiful colors.
I flip and flutter, dip and dance, decorating daisies, pirouetting on petunias, then resting on roses.

Now, I know what you are thinking: Predators can catch me quite easily. True, but they don't.
Do you know why? Because they think I am poisonous. Let me tell you a secret:
I'm not, but my colors are similar to a butterfly that *is* poisonous.

So predators leave me alone                                        gracefully
                                    .    free to  .   ·                        ·  .    flutter by.

# EASTERN SPINY SOFTSHELL TURTLE

Boy, oh, boy! It sure feels good to get all cleaned up! I'm usually covered with mud. Living in rivers, I swim to the bottom and wiggle and diggle. *Diggle* is a word I made up. I dig a bit and wiggle a bit. After wiggling and diggling, I lie half-buried on the river bottom, blending in.

My shell's so flat that no one notices me, and the pattern on my back matches the mud, sand, and pebbles. Predators can't spot me easily. . . and neither can the small animals that I prey upon. I wait patiently for insects, snails, crayfish, frogs, and fish to come along. Then I extend my long neck and grab them.

Well, I've been cleaned up long enough. It's time for me to wiggle and diggle!

# RED-EYED VIREO

Mom didn't think I was ready to leave the nest . . .

but I wanted to fly! You see, my brothers and sisters,
we broke out of our eggshells and ate so many
insects that our wings grew and our feathers filled
in and, well, I thought I could really fly.

So, out of the nest I jumped . . . .

I flapped and flapped as hard as I could.
*I was flying!* But then my wings got all
mixed up, and

      I

             tumbled

                   down.

Mom's a little upset,
but she's still feeding me.
She said I flew pretty well.

# EASTERN BOX TURTLE

So, you want to know the secrets to a long life. After fifty years, I'd say it's pretty simple: *eat*, *sleep*, *crawl*, *hide*, *share*, and *have fun!*

I *eat* almost anything: worms, snails, insects, berries, fungi. I *sleep* in the dirt at night and hibernate underground in the winter, so I'm always rarin' to go. Good sleep lets me *crawl* miles and miles through the woods each year. When in danger, I *hide*. My shell is hinged on the bottom, so I just pull my legs, head, and tail back inside and snap it shut. I'm not territorial, so I *share* my woods, and sometimes the spots where I hibernate, with other box turtles. And I always *have fun*. I enjoy bathing in puddles, and I love wallowing in mud!

# SPOTTED SALAMANDER

Rain, Rain

*Rain, rain, won't you stay?*
*Keep my skin moist every day.*
*I will find a pool and lay*
*lots of watery eggs today.*

*Swim, swim, as larvae.*
*Use your gills or skin to breathe.*
*Then grow fingers, lungs, and feet.*
*Life on land is just as neat!*

# MONARCH

I have been watching the most amazing thing: One of my caterpillar friends just changed shape completely. He called it *metamorphosis*.

You see, a few days ago, after weeks of munching milkweed, he just stopped eating and attached himself upside down to a leaf. Then he shed his old skin, and the new skin underneath was green! It hardened, forming a protective covering. He said he was a *chrysalis*.

This morning his covering turned clear like a window, and guess what? I could see inside: He was orange and black. And he didn't look like a caterpillar anymore.

It's the most curious thing: A few minutes ago, he broke out of his covering, and he's a butterfly now. He said that I, too, will change into a butterfly soon, a beautiful monarch butterfly, just like him.

I guess life is all about change, and *change looks good!*

# CURIOUS CRITTERS: NATURAL HISTORY

**American bullfrogs,** the largest frogs in North America, can jump as far as six feet. During breeding season, males choose prime egg-laying areas, call to females, and defend their territories by wrestling with other males. Bullfrogs are nocturnal hunters and eat nearly any animal that can fit into their mouths, including small birds.

**Ohio crawfish,** a particular species of crayfish, live in cool streams and ponds. Crayfish—known regionally as crawdads, crawfish, or mud-bugs—have many pairs of appendages, including a pair of chelipeds (with large claws, or chelae) in the front, medium-sized walking legs in the middle, and small swimmerets under the tail. Any of these can be regenerated if injured. Crayfish cannot turn their heads; instead, their eyestalks bend. Long antennae help them navigate in the mud.

**Big brown bats,** zipping around at speeds up to forty miles per hour, use echolocation and sharp teeth to catch insects. A single big brown bat weighs about as much as three U.S. quarters. While most small animals have relatively short life spans, these mammals live up to eighteen years. With strong homing abilities, they return to the same roosts year after year.

**American toads** swim in shallow waters as tadpoles and hop on land as adults. These amphibians have dry, bumpy skin in comparison to the smooth, wet skin of frogs. Large parotoid glands behind their eyes produce a toxin that tastes bitter to predators. With their sticky tongues, American toads can catch hundreds of insects per day.

**Goldfish,** members of the minnow family, were bred by the Chinese over 1,000 years ago. By repeatedly mating brilliantly colored male and female minnows, the Chinese produced increasingly colorful off-spring. Today there are over 100 types of goldfish. In the wild, gold-fish eat crustaceans, insects, and aquatic plants. Many goldfish owners supplement fish flakes with green peas, worms, or other foods. Able to recognize people, goldfish often get excited when their owners visit.

**Fox snakes** are constrictors, using their strong abdominal muscles to subdue prey by encircling and squeezing. When bothered, they may release an unpleasant odor from scent glands near the tail. Although generally docile, bold coloration and the tendency to vibrate their tails when disturbed cause many people to mistake fox snakes for rattle-snakes.

**Blue jays** are great vocalists, making a wide variety of sounds, includ-ing their signature "jay-jay" call. They can imitate a variety of bird sounds, frequently those of hawks. Blue jays live in many different habitats, from forests to suburbs. They eat nuts, insects, and occasion-ally eggs of other birds. Quite aggressive, blue jays drive other birds from feeders.

**Southern flying squirrels** use their tails as rudders to guide them when they glide. The large eyes of these high-energy mammals enable them to search at night for food, including nuts, fungi, fruits, flowers, in-sects, bird eggs, nestlings, small mammals, and carrion. Rarely seen unless by spotlight, southern flying squirrels are often heard making high-pitched squeaks.

**Eastern screech-owls** are often heard making trilling calls just after sunset. Mates, which typically stay together for life, call to one another. Eastern screech-owls use cavities in trees for nests and easily adapt to living in nesting boxes. They are one of the most common owls in North America.

**Gray treefrogs** live in trees and shrubs most of the year, migrating to woodland ponds and flooded farm fields in the spring for reproduction. In colder areas, they can survive winter by becoming partially frozen. While heart and lung functions cease and brain activity nearly stops, gray treefrogs return to full vitality upon thawing. Some people say they can predict rain by listening for the trilling of gray treefrogs.

**Jumping spiders** stalk animals, leaping as much as twenty-five times the length of their bodies in order to capture prey. As they jump, these arachnids spin silk threads, which act as safety ropes. Jumping spiders are quite curious: When approached, they turn to face visitors head-on and inspect them closely.

**Red-eyed vireos** build their nests in forked tree branches using plant material and spider webs. Young fledge ten to twelve days after hatching, and adults continue to feed them for another week or two. Red-eyed vireos slurringly sing "*sewee, seewit, seeowit, seeyee,*" their pitch rising and falling as if repeatedly asking questions and then answering. A single bird can repeat this call more than 20,000 times in one day!

**Bush katydids,** usually green, are occasionally pink, orange, or yellow. Scientists don't know how often these recessive traits appear, but it's safe to say they are extremely rare. Despite their family name, not all katydids make the famous "Katy did. Katy didn't." call. Bush katydids make a variety of other sounds, singing both day and night.

**Red flat bark beetles** crawl under the bark of trees, both as larvae and as adults. The larvae hunt for other beetles and their larvae; the adults, however, forage for plant material and fungi. As with many other types of beetles, they are often spotted with mites hitching rides. These arachnids usually cause no problems other than slowing the beetles down.

**Eastern box turtles** may live a long time. One female in Massachusetts is over 150 years old. The turtles' unique box-like shells are covered with keratin—the material found in human fingernails—and may re grow if damaged. In the wild, Eastern box turtles do not mate until after ten years of age, with most offspring not surviving to produce young. Collecting, along with habitat destruction, have put many populations near the brink of collapse.

**Virginia opossums,** among the oldest mammals on Earth, have been around since the dinosaurs. Females carry their underdeveloped young in a pouch called a marsupium until they mature. Virginia opossums use their prehensile tails for grasping and briefly hanging upside down. When disturbed, they often behave in a way that makes them appear dead, which is the source of the expression "play possum." The name "opossum," derived from an Indian word, is often shortened to "possum."

**Black swallowtails** benefit from looking like their toxic relatives, pipevine swallowtails. Poisonous animals are often brightly colored, warning predators to stay away. Black swallowtail caterpillars generally feed on plants in the parsley family, including carrots and Queen Anne's lace. When black swallowtails pupate, their chrysalises vary in color according to locality, allowing them to be camouflaged in different environments.

**Spotted salamanders** are seldom seen throughout the year, but in the spring they migrate by the hundreds to vernal pools, basins that temporarily fill with water. There they dance at night, looking for mates. After egg-laying, adults leave the pool, and larvae begin to develop. As summer heat dries their pools, the larvae metamorphose and crawl into woodlands. Most adults return each spring to their ancestral vernal pools.

**Chinese praying mantises** originated in China but are now common in many parts of North America, thanks mainly to gardeners, who introduced the species to help control insect pests. Chinese mantises have huge appetites, eating all kinds of insects as well as small amphibians, reptiles, and even birds. Females lay several oothecae, which are hard, foam-like cases, containing about 200 eggs. These oothecae are available in gardening stores.

**Eastern spiny softshell turtles** can breathe two ways. In shallow waters, they extend their long necks, sticking their noses just above the surface. They can also breathe underwater by drawing water into the mouth and pharynx, where linings absorb dissolved oxygen and release carbon dioxide, allowing the reptiles to remain submerged for long periods of time. Eastern spiny softshell turtles are most easily seen atop partially submerged logs, where they bask in the sun.

**Monarch** caterpillars feed on milkweed leaves, but, as they grow, they shed their skins and eat them, too. When fully grown, larvae attach themselves to their milkweed plants, hang upside down, and molt once more. Their new skins turn green and harden, forming protective cases. The monarchs are now in the form of chrysalises. In about two weeks the chrysalises become transparent, a sign that butterflies will soon emerge.

# CURIOUS CRITTERS
## LIFE-SIZE SILHOUETTES

1

2

3

Can you identify the animals?

6

4

One animal's shape has changed. Which one?

7

9

10

5

8

11

14

19

15

12

16

How many animals' silhouettes have been reversed? Which ones?

13

17

What do the silhouette colors mean?

20

Answers are on the next page.

18

21

# GLOSSARY

**Amphibian:** an animal that lives both in water and on land, typically in water as a larva and, after metamorphosis, on land as an adult.

**Antenna:** one of a pair of sensory appendages on the heads of insects, crustaceans, and other arthropods.

**Arachnid:** spiders, mites, and other eight-legged animals of the class *Arachnida*.

**Camouflage:** to hide by matching the appearance of one's surroundings.

**Caterpillar:** the larva of either a butterfly or moth.

**Chrysalis:** a butterfly pupa, which is covered with a hardened, protective case.

**Constrictor:** a snake that kills its prey by squeezing.

**Echolocation:** perception through emitting sounds and measuring the time it takes for the sounds to reflect back from objects.

**Fledge:** to leave the nest after developing feathers for flight.

**Gill:** an organ used by some aquatic animals for breathing.

**Gland:** an organ that produces substances that are released from the body or into the bloodstream.

**Hibernation:** a resting state for animals used to survive winter.

**Keratin:** the fibrous protein found in vertebrates that makes up a number of protective structures, including hair, nails, hooves, horns, and the outer material on most turtle shells.

**Larva:** the juvenile stage of life, after emergence from an egg and before metamorphosis into a pupa, for animals undergoing incomplete metamorphosis, such as insects and amphibians; plural, larvae.

**Mammal:** a warm-blooded animal of the class *Mammalia* sharing certain traits, such as hair and milk-producing glands.

**Marsupial:** a mammal whose young are born prematurely and then nursed in their mother's front pouch, or marsupium, until they fully develop.

**Metamorphosis:** for animals, a change in bodily form through growth and restructuring.

**Migrate:** to move temporarily, often seasonally, from one region or climate to another that is more favorable for feeding or breeding.

**Mite:** a small arachnid, which may be parasitic upon animals or feed on plants; some live freely in the soil.

**Nocturnal:** active at night.

**Omnivore:** an animal that eats all kinds of foods, not just animals or plants.

**Pharynx:** the passageway between the cavities of the mouth and nose and the esophagus.

**Predator:** an animal that hunts other animals.

**Prey:** an animal hunted by other animals

**Pupa:** the stage, after larva and before adult, in the life cycle of insects that undergo complete metamorphosis.

**Recessive Trait:** a genetically determined characteristic only observed in the presence of two gene variants; often found in a small portion of a population.

**Rodent:** a group of smallish mammals with continuously growing front teeth, which are used for gnawing.

**Tadpole:** the common name for a frog or toad larva.

**Toxin:** a poisonous substance that causes harm to a living organism.

**Trill:** a vibrating or rapidly pulsing sound, similar to the sound of a police whistle.

**Vernal Pool:** a temporary body of water, filling in late winter or spring, and serving as a fishless breeding habitat.

**Answer Key to Silhouette Pages:** 1. Virginia Opossum, 2. Eastern Box Turtle, 3. Chinese Praying Mantis, 4. American Bullfrog, 5. Jumping Spider, 6. Blue Jay, 7. Eastern Spiny Softshell Turtle (Juvenile), 8. Red Flat Bark Beetle, 9. American Toad, 10. Big Brown Bat, 11. Bush Katydid, 12. Red-Eyed Vireo (Fledgling), 13. Ohio Crawfish, 14. Black Swallowtail, 15. Goldfish, 16. Fox Snake, 17. Gray Treefrog, 18. Monarch (Larva), 19. Eastern Screech-Owl, 20. Southern Flying Squirrel, 21. Spotted Salamander

The Fox Snake's shape changed.

Four animals' silhouettes have been reversed: Jumping Spider, Black Swallowtail, Monarch, and Southern Flying Squirrel.

## Silhouette Color Groupings:

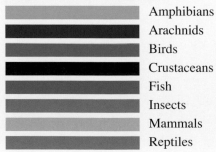

| | |
|---|---|
| | Amphibians |
| | Arachnids |
| | Birds |
| | Crustaceans |
| | Fish |
| | Insects |
| | Mammals |
| | Reptiles |

**Extra Challenge:** Can you identify the Curious Critters not labled in this book? You can find the answers on page two.

More Curious Critters are on the way! Games, educational resources, and additional photos at *www.curious-critters.com*